DISCOVERING THE TECHNOLOGY OF
ANCIENT GREECE

LINDSEY LOWE

Cavendish
Square

Published in 2024 by Cavendish Square Publishing, LLC
2544 Clinton Street, Buffalo, NY 14224

Portions of this work were originally authored by Charlie Samuels and published as *Technology in Ancient Greece*. All new material this edition authored by Lindsey Lowe.

Website: cavendishsq.com

This publication represents the opinions and views of the author based on his or her personal experience, knowledge, and research. The information in this book serves as a general guide only. The author and publisher have used their best efforts in preparing this book and disclaim liability rising directly or indirectly from the use and application of this book.

All websites were available and accurate when this book was sent to press.

Children's Publisher: Anne O'Daly
Design Manager: Keith Davis
Designer: Lynne Lennon
Picture Manager: Sophie Mortimer

Picture Credits
Front Cover: Shutterstock: RHIMAE br, tilialucida t.
Alamy: Ancient Art & Architecture 34; Peter Horree: 42; Corbis: Bettmann 35; Public Domain: Marie-Lan Nguyen 43; Shutterstock: 24, George W. Bailey 27, Anton Balash 14, Panos Karos 17, Karl Allen Lugmayer 38, polarterm 1, 13 Ivelin Radkov 37, Alexander a. Trofimov 6, Marek Uliasz 25; Thinkstock/istockphoto: 5, 7, 23, 36; Photos.com: 20, 22, 32, 33, 35.

Cataloging-in-Publication Data

Names: Lowe, Lindsey.
Title: Discovering the technology of ancient Greece / Lindsey Lowe.
Description: Buffalo, New York : Cavendish Square Publishing, 2024. |
    Series: Discovering ancient technology | Includes glossary and index.
Identifiers: ISBN 9781502669391 (pbk.) | ISBN 9781502669407 (library bound) |
    ISBN 9781502669414 (ebook)
Subjects: LCSH: Technology--Greece--History--Juvenile literature. | Science--Greece--History--
    Juvenile literature. | Greece--Civilization--Juvenile literature. | Greece--History--To 146 B.C.--
    Juvenile literature.
Classification: LCC T16.L69 2024 | DDC 609.38--dc23

CPSIA compliance information: Batch #CSCSQ24: For further information contact Cavendish Square Publishing LLC at 1-877-980-4450.

Printed in the United States of America

Find us on

CONTENTS

INTRODUCTION

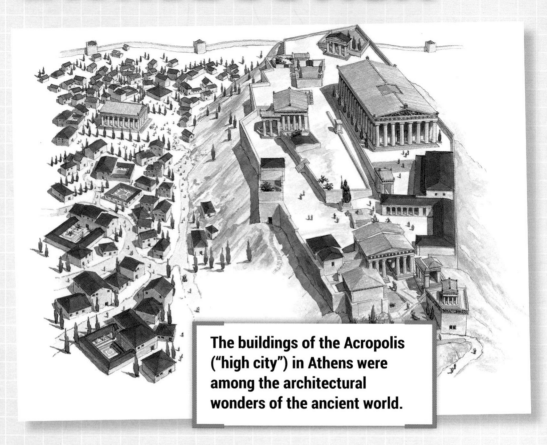

The buildings of the Acropolis ("high city") in Athens were among the architectural wonders of the ancient world.

People have been living in Greece for thousands of years. However, there was never a single country called "ancient Greece." It was a collection of city-states that ruled themselves. The ancient Greeks had an insatiable thirst for knowledge. While technology improved in relatively small steps, Greek scientists tried to understand how and why things happened. They enjoyed learning as an intellectual challenge. The advances that ancient Greeks made in political thinking, science, philosophy, math, and art helped to shape the entire Western world.

WARRING STATES

Ancient Greece was not united. It was a series of city-states that often fought, but which all shared a similar culture and worshiped the same gods. The two most powerful city-states were Athens and Sparta. They were often at war, but sometimes made alliances to fight when threatened by countries such as Persia. This book introduces readers to the most important examples of the technology behind this remarkable period of intellectual development.

A developed writing system allowed the Greeks to record the results of their studies, particularly in philosophy and math.

TECHNICAL KNOW-HOW

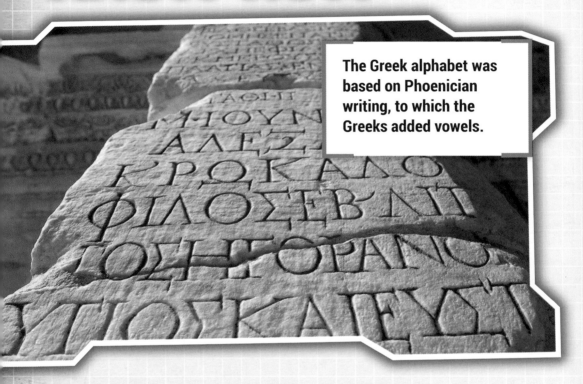

The Greek alphabet was based on Phoenician writing, to which the Greeks added vowels.

The ancient Greeks lived in the lands around southeastern Europe along the coasts of the Mediterranean Sea. These were regions that had been influenced by a number of earlier peoples. The Greeks were able to adopt some of the achievements of these other cultures. The ancient Egyptians had invented papyrus, which the Greeks used to write on.

In the Greek Bronze Age, the Minoans of Crete created a complex plumbing system to provide water for bathing.

The Phoenician alphabet was the basis of Greek writing. The Greeks also used coinage invented in Lydia, in modern-day Turkey, and improved upon it. They built magnificent temples and public buildings from marble, but their private homes were made from the same mud bricks used by other cultures in the region. The Greeks used plumbing, and understood the importance of clean water for health.

LEARNING

Unlike other peoples, however, the Greeks enjoyed learning for its own sake. They created the first public library at Alexandria to share knowledge. Careful observations were the foundation of modern astronomy and medicine, and their ways of thinking about the world's mysteries were the basis of modern philosophy.

FARMING

A farmer uses oxen to plow a field. In the background, workers harvest olives next to rows of grapevines.

Eighty percent of the population worked on the land. People produced more food than they needed. This was traded across the Mediterranean. Farming was hard work as the soil was poor and the land was often hilly. The staple foods were cereals, grapes, and olives, which all needed plenty of sun but could grow without much water.

Greek farmers plowed their fields twice a year: in spring and in the fall. Their plows were made from wood, and sometimes tipped with iron. Farmers built terraces on the sides of hills to increase the amount of land they could plant. They used irrigation and crop rotation to improve the poor soil.

FOOD SUPPLIES

Barley was grown between the rows of olive trees. Fish was also an important part of the diet, and fish were caught on lines using bronze fishhooks. Wealthy people hunted wild deer, boar, and hare using bows and arrows, nets, and traps.

TECHNICAL SPECS

» Olives were harvested by beating the olive tree with whiplike branches until the fruit dropped to the ground.

» Olive oil was used for cooking and eating, but also as a fuel for lamps and as a kind of soap.

» The Greeks made wine by stomping on grapes. The wine was so thick it had to be strained using a bronze strainer. It was usually diluted with water.

» Raisins were made by letting grapes dry in the sun.

» Farmers kept goats to use for milk and cheese as well as wool.

» Greece exported wine and olive oil. By producing a surplus, the ancient Greeks were able to become a powerful trading nation.

Olive trees grow easily in Greece, despite the poor soil, mountainous landscape, and dry climate.

CONSTRUCTION

Homes in ancient Greece were usually built from sun-dried mud bricks. For this reason, very little remains of this domestic architecture. However, temples and other magnificent public buildings were constructed from marble. Many of these buildings remain reasonably intact today.

HOUSE AT OLYNTHOS

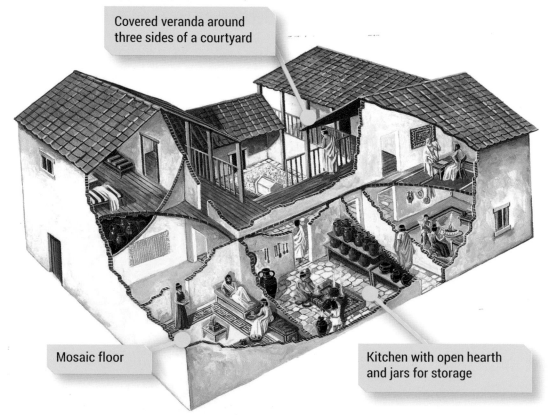

Covered veranda around three sides of a courtyard

Mosaic floor

Kitchen with open hearth and jars for storage

ACROPOLIS, ATHENS

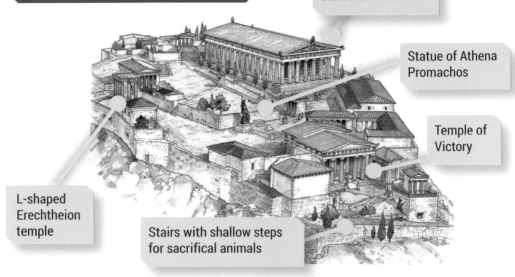

Parthenon housing statue of Athena

Statue of Athena Promachos

Temple of Victory

L-shaped Erechtheion temple

Stairs with shallow steps for sacrifical animals

The earliest type of ancient Greek house dates from around 1800 B.C.E. It had a main room or hall, called a megaron, with a hearth and columns to support the roof. From the fifth century B.C.E., houses were built around an open courtyard designed to keep the house cool in the hot summers. There was also a covered veranda along three sides of the courtyard to give shade.

FLOOR DECORATIONS

Floors were finished off with mosaic tiles in the homes of the wealthy. In more modest homes, the bare earth was probably just plastered or left completely undecorated.

TECHNICAL SPECS

» Wood was only used for doors, window shutters, and roofs, because there was a shortage of suitable trees for building.

» The Greek city of Olynthos was destroyed on the orders of Philip of Macedonia in 348 B.C.E. Its ruins revealed the remains of ancient Greek homes.

» Houses in Olynthos were built in rows on a grid system.

» Women were kept out of view. Their quarters were as far as possible from doors or windows that opened onto the street.

» Bricks for building houses were shaped from mud and left in the sun to dry.

TEMPLES AND THE PARTHENON

THE PARTHENON

The Parthenon was built on the Acropolis ("high city") in Athens. It housed a giant statue of the goddess Athena, made by the sculptor Pheidias.

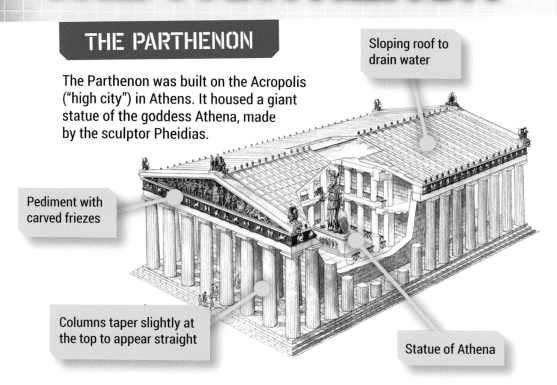

Sloping roof to drain water

Pediment with carved friezes

Columns taper slightly at the top to appear straight

Statue of Athena

The architecture of ancient Greece reached its peak in its temples. The most important building in Athens was the Parthenon, which stood on the Acropolis, a rocky hill overlooking the city. It was built for the goddess Athena. Its magnificent marble columns made this type of building a template for other public buildings.

Marble was plentiful in Greece. It was quarried by masons who hammered wooden wedges into cracks in the rock, then soaked them with water. As the wet wood expanded, the marble cracked. The blocks were shaped in the quarry but were finely carved at the building site. They fit together so well that no mortar was needed.

COLUMNS

Greek architecture is famous for its columns. Columns were made from short, round cylinders of marble. To make a column, a number of cylinders were pinned together using metal clips. Ropes and pulleys raised the column into place.

TECHNICAL SPECS

» The Greeks used a form of skylight. They placed tiles of very thin marble in roofs to let the light through.

» Doric columns were plain at the capital (top); Ionic columns had rams-horn curls; Corinthian columns were decorated with carvings of acanthus leaves.

» The ancient Greeks used an optical illusion in the columns at the Parthenon. From a distance, straight columns look as though they bend outward. To compensate for this, the Greeks made them taper slightly toward the top so that they appeared straight.

» Rainwater drained off temple roofs through spouts carved in the shape of animal heads.

» Decorative friezes were often added to the fronts of temples.

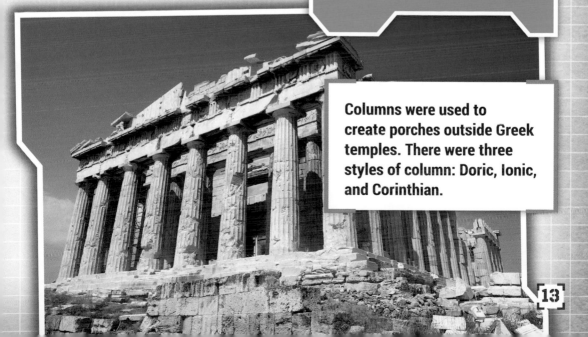

Columns were used to create porches outside Greek temples. There were three styles of column: Doric, Ionic, and Corinthian.

SCULPTURE

Most sculptures in ancient Greece were made for temples dedicated to a specific god or goddess. Other sculptures were made to decorate public buildings. They were made from limestone, marble, or bronze. These materials are hard-wearing and some statues and parts of friezes survive today.

This marble statue of the god Apollo was carved early in the second century C.E. It was a copy of a much earlier statue.

TECHNICAL SPECS

» Friezes were long, narrow bands of relief carvings that decorated the upper walls of Greek temples.

» Friezes, such as the one on the Parthenon in Athens, were painted with bright colors.

» Statues were finished with metal attachments, such as spears, swords, bridles, and other decorations such as women's jewelry.

» Bronze statues were finished using glass for eyes, copper for lips, and silver for teeth and fingernails.

» Humans and gods were carved at the same size. Male statues were usually young and often carved nude to show the Greek idea of the perfect human form.

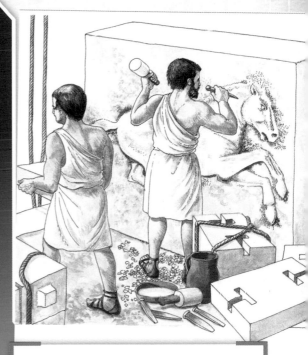

A worker carves a horse for a frieze. The blocks of marble were held together by pieces of metal inserted in the T-shaped holes.

To make a sculpture, a sculptor first created a full-size model in clay. The marble was chiseled into a rough form copying the shape of the clay model. A master sculptor then finished the carving. The surface was smoothed before it was painted.

BRONZES

Bronze statues were cast using the lost wax method. A wax model was covered with clay, then baked hard. The wax melted and was poured out of the mold, which was filled with molten metal and left to harden. When the clay was broken off it revealed the bronze statue.

THEATERS

The semicircular space in a Greek theater was known as the orchestra. The chorus performed dances there.

Almost every Greek city had an open-air theater in which plays were performed during the day. These plays were either tragedies or comedies and were often staged as part of religious festivals. In Athens, dramas in honor of Dionysus, the god of wine, resembled modern plays. The theaters were feats of acoustic engineering.

Theaters were built on hillsides. They were shaped like horseshoes, with steps cut into the hillside for seating. The flat area at the bottom was called the orchestra. It held the circular stage.

ACOUSTICS

A theater could seat up to 18,000 people, and the people in back had to be able to hear the actors as well as the people in the front row could. The Greeks used math to work out the best acoustics. In the theater at Epidaurus, which is still used today, speech from the stage is amplified by the bowl-like effect of the hillside.

TECHNICAL SPECS

» Actors entered the orchestra via a tall arched entrance called a parodoi or eisodoi.

» The seats in the front rows were wooden, so they could be removed; the rest were stone. The best seats at the front were reserved for officials, visitors, and competition judges.

» Stone tokens were used as tickets. They were marked with seat numbers.

» Special effects included a crane (*mechane*) that made it look as though the actor was flying, and trapdoors in the floor were used to bring actors onto the stage.

» From 465 B.C.E., a scenic wall was hung or stood behind the orchestra. Death scenes always took place behind this skene (from which the modern word "scene" comes).

Masks were worn to impress or frighten the audience. They also meant the same performers could play different characters.

SCIENCE AND INVENTION

The ancient Greeks enjoyed philosophy—the study of ideas. But around the sixth century B.C.E., their observations of the world allowed them to separate philosophy from science. Their studies taught them, for example, that sickness was often caused by bad hygiene, not by the gods, as had been thought. The Greeks began to rethink how they looked at the world.

The School of Athens, painted by Raphael in 1510, shows famous Greek philosophers, with Plato and Aristotle in the center.

TECHNICAL SPECS

» The Antikythera mechanism was found in 1900 in an ancient shipwreck. It took scientists a century to realize that it was a computer made up of a series of different-sized wheels.

» Heron of Alexandria invented the world's first slot machine. It was used at temples to dispense holy water for washing as a person entered the temple.

» Heron also invented the first simple steam engine. A pot filled with water was placed over a fire. Two tubes carried steam into a hollow metal ball, where it flowed out through two angled tubes. That made the ball rotate.

This steam engine was invented by Heron. Steam expelled from the bent tubes rotated the ball.

Although the Greeks attempted to understand more about the world, they did not write down many of their discoveries. As a result, historians once believed that the ancient Greeks had not been interested in science.

INVENTIONS

Today we know this belief was wrong. For example, the Greeks developed the world's first computer. The so-called Antikythera mechanism was probably used to calculate the movements of the sun and moon. Other Greek inventions included the steam engine and the slot machine. The Greeks were inquisitive and loved knowledge. They opened the first public library in Egypt in the third century B.C.E. It was part of the Museum of Alexandria, which was an early kind of research institute.

ARCHIMEDES

One of the weapons said to have been built by Archimedes to defend Syracuse was a lens that focused the sun's rays to set fire to enemy ships.

Archimedes was a prolific inventor. He was also one of the greatest mathematicians who ever lived. He believed that everything in life could be based on numbers. Many of his discoveries are still in use today. Schoolchildren use one of them daily without realizing it: he calculated the value of pi in order to work out the area of a circle.

Archimedes was not the first person to use levers, but he was the first person to understand the principle behind them. He calculated the length of lever needed to move any object. He used a lever to lift a ship out of a dry dock and into the sea.

WEAPONS

Archimedes invented several weapons to protect his city of Syracuse from a Roman attack. He redesigned the city walls to accommodate large wooden cranes that dropped huge boulders onto the enemy. Another weapon, the "claw," grabbed enemy ships and lifted them out of the water, overturning them.

TECHNICAL SPECS

» Archimedes's claw was probably a crane with a grappling hook.

» Archimedes is said to have invented the first fire engine, a cart that carried water.

» Archimedes discovered the principle of the displacement of water when he got into a full bath and it overflowed.

» King Hieron was worried that his gold crown had been mixed with cheaper silver. Silver weighs less than gold. Archimedes measured the water displaced by the crown against the water displaced by a solid gold object of the same weight. He was able to prove that the king had indeed been duped.

HOW TO...

The Archimedes screw pump was a large spiral screw inside a cylinder. As the screw was turned, it raised the water from one level to another by pushing it against the side of the cylinder. The ancient Egyptians used the screw to raise water from the Nile for the irrigation of crops. The screw is still used in many parts of the world.

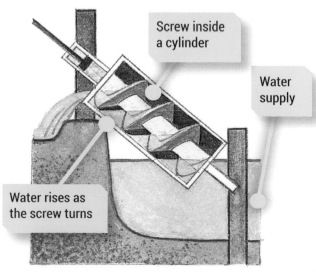

Screw inside a cylinder

Water supply

Water rises as the screw turns

ARISTOTLE

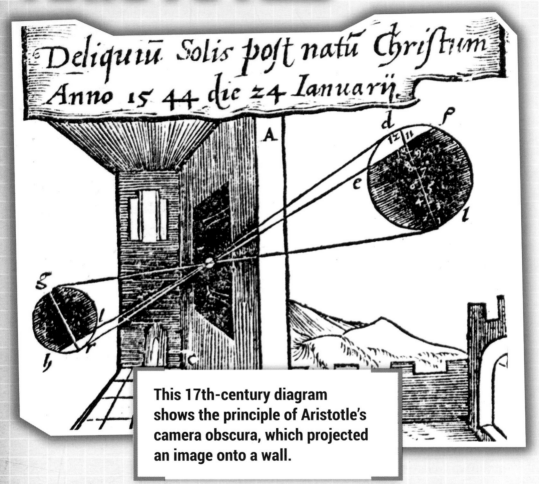

Deliquiũ Solis poſt natũ Chriſtum Anno 15 44 die 24 Ianuarÿ.

This 17th-century diagram shows the principle of Aristotle's camera obscura, which projected an image onto a wall.

Aristotle was perhaps the greatest thinker of all time. His work covered every subject of study known in ancient Greece, including politics, logic, meteorology, physics, and theology. His work has influenced almost every area of modern thought and the camera obscura he invented is still used today.

Aristotle tried to separate philosophy from science. He was the first person to spell out that science is based on careful observation. Aristotle proved that the Earth is round by observing the curved shadow it cast on the moon during a lunar eclipse.

EARTH SCIENCE

Aristotle estimated the diameter of the Earth to within 50 percent of its true value. He observed that, as he traveled north or south, new stars appeared on one horizon while others fell below the other horizon. This happened after even a short distance, showing that the Earth was not very big.

TECHNICAL SPECS

» Aristotle believed that matter was composed of four elements: earth, air, water, and fire. He also said the heavens were made of a fifth element, "aether."

» Aristotle believed that the heavens were perfect and unchanging, while Earth was subject to change.

» Aristotle's observations set the standard for future scientific study. He was one of the first to collect plant specimens and classify them into groups.

» The camera obscura was the forerunner of the modern camera. It was a light-tight box with a small hole in one side. Light from the hole formed an inverted image on the opposite side. The device allowed eclipses to be observed safely.

Aristotle was a founder of Western philosophy. He studied with Plato and taught the young Alexander the Great.

PYTHAGORAS

Pythagoras was a Greek mathematician, astronomer, and philosopher. He is most famous for the Pythagorean theorem, which is still used in classrooms to help calculate right-angled triangles.

Pythagoras had many followers. They all settled in a Greek colony in southern Italy. Pythagoras greatly influenced the younger Greek philosopher, Plato. In turn, Plato influenced generations of later philosophers. The followers of Pythagoras were known as the Pythagoreans. They believed that the Earth was a sphere at the center of a spherical universe.

In this medieval drawing, Pythagoras tests the sounds produced by different-sized bells and glasses containing different amounts of liquid.

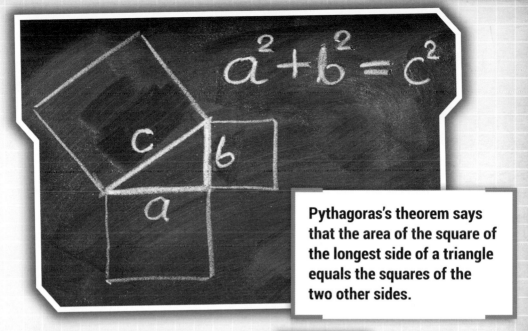

$$a^2 + b^2 = c^2$$

c

b

a

Pythagoras's theorem says that the area of the square of the longest side of a triangle equals the squares of the two other sides.

They believed that the planets sat in their own transparent spheres, and that these spheres were spaced out evenly and rotated around Earth.

MATH IS ALL

Pythagoras believed the whole world could be understood through math. He saw a particularly close link between music and math. He discovered that the intervals between musical notes could be expressed in mathematical terms. Apart from his theorem, Pythagoras's main contribution to science was the realization that answers to scientific problems usually led to new problems.

TECHNICAL SPECS

» Pythagoras's theorem is about the shape and area of right-angled triangles. The theory had been known to the Sumerians and to the ancient Chinese, but the Greek thinker proved it was right.

» Pythagoras described square numbers and cubic numbers before they were fully understood.

» The Pythagoreans treated men and women equally, which was unknown in ancient Greece.

» Pythagoras left no original writings, so everything we know about him comes from his disciples and his critics.

TRANSPORT

CARGO SHIP

Ancient Greece relied on shipping to communicate with its many islands and to carry trade goods and settlers throughout the Mediterranean. Earlier vessels had curved prows and one row of oars.

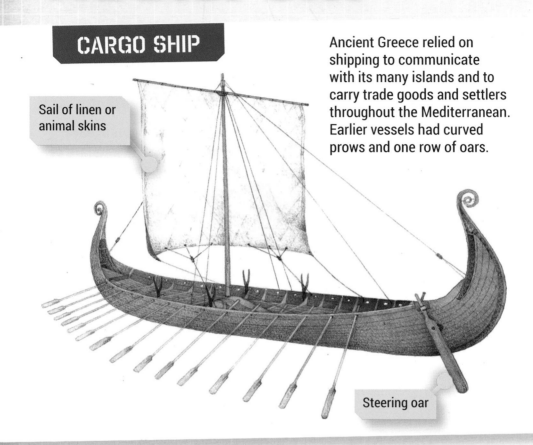

Sail of linen or animal skins

Steering oar

The Greek mainland and islands are surrounded by water. The land is mountainous, and the ancient Greeks had few roads. They mainly traveled by ship. When they traveled on land, it was usually on foot. The thinker Socrates once walked from Athens to Olympia, a total of 200 miles (320 km), in five or six days.

ON LAND

A cart track allowed goods to be carried the 5 miles (8 km) between the port of Piraeus and Athens. Chariots were used for short journeys; for longer distances some people went by mule. Horses were rarely used: the Greeks had no saddles, stirrups, or horseshoes. The Greeks built a railway, Dioklos, that ran 4 miles (6.4 km) across the Isthmus of Corinth. This was a major engineering achievement. It meant small warships or empty cargo vessels could be pulled across the isthmus rather than having to sail around the peninsula.

PHAROS

Mirror reflected sunlight during the day

Furnace produced flames to burn at night

Built of limestone blocks

Foundation platform

TECHNICAL SPECS

» Sea travel was dangerous because of pirates, bad weather, and poor navigation. The Greeks built the world's first lighthouse (Pharos) at Alexandria to guide ships safely into the harbor.

» The Dioklos railway was a paved road of limestone blocks. Two parallel grooves 5 feet (1.5 m) apart held the wheels of trolleys pushed by slaves.

» The ancient Greeks greatly improved upon Babylonian maps. They invented both latitude and longitude and the major lines of latitude, such as the equator, the Tropic of Cancer, and the Tropic of Capricorn.

TRIREMES

Athens was the most powerful of the Greek city-states. The Athenians called their navy their "wooden walls." By controlling the Aegean Sea, the Athenians dictated which goods and which troops went to and from the islands. The warships, triremes, also protected merchant vessels from attack as they brought food and luxuries to the Athenian port of Piraeus.

A trireme rams an enemy vessel. Triremes had a few armed soldiers on deck ready to board a rammed ship.

CROSS-SECTION

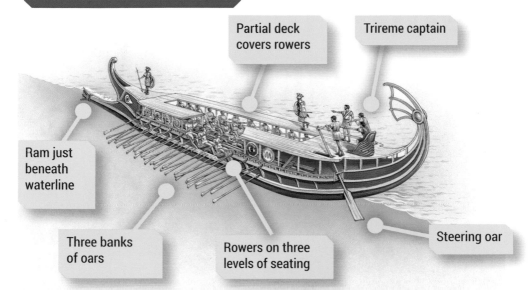

Partial deck covers rowers

Trireme captain

Ram just beneath waterline

Three banks of oars

Rowers on three levels of seating

Steering oar

The ancient Greeks had one type of warship: the trireme. This wooden galley was powered by up to 170 oarsmen sitting in three rows. At its most powerful, the city-state of Athens had 400 triremes in service.

RAMMING

At its bow, below the waterline, the trireme had a long wooden ram covered in bronze. To sink an enemy ship, the trireme would ram it in the side. If the enemy boat did not sink, soldiers boarded it. Crews spent long periods practicing ramming and boarding maneuvers.

TECHNICAL SPECS

» The name trireme comes from the three banks of oars.

» Triremes dominated the Mediterranean between the seventh and fourth centuries B.C.E.

» A piper or drummer sometimes played a beat on the trireme to keep the rowing in time.

» Three main types of wood were used in construction: fir, pine, and cedar. Oak was used for the hulls. The ships had to be light enough to be carried ashore.

» In favorable sailing conditions, a trireme could cover up to 60 miles (96 km) in a day.

WARFARE AND WEAPONS

Hoplites fought in close formations known as phalanxes. Their shields overlapped to form a wall.

The ancient Greek city-states were often at war. It was normal for Greek men to join an army. Boys between the ages of 18 and 20 were automatically trained as soldiers in readiness for being called to war. In Sparta, the organization of the whole state was based on warfare. Hoplite warriors controlled the land; the trireme controlled the seas.

Between the seventh and fourth centuries B.C.E., the hoplite dominated warfare. Hoplites came from wealthy families, who paid for their own armor and weapons. Poorer soldiers often served as archers and stone-slingers.

SIEGE WARFARE

Sieges were an important part of warfare. Armies used catapults, flamethrowers, and stone-slingers to defeat a walled city. The defenders dropped cauldrons of burning coals and sulfur on attackers.

TECHNICAL SPECS

» The breastplate consisted of two metal plates joined at the sides by leather straps. The sides of the upper body were left unprotected.

» Helmets were vital, because when hoplites marched in a phalanx, their heads were left exposed to the enemy.

» Military commanders were called strategoi, the source of the English word "strategy."

» Cavalrymen would not willingly charge a phalanx as they and the horses risked being speared.

» Phalanxes tried to break a gap in the opposing phalanx to attack the enemy's flanks and rear.

» Shields had extra strength from the loop for the hoplite's arm. There was also a handle to grip.

Spartan hoplites prepare to raid enemy territory. Sparta was the most warlike of the ancient Greek city-states.

ASTRONOMY

The ancient Greeks contributed to our understanding of astronomy, the study of heavenly bodies. The Greeks were the first people to realize Earth is a sphere, and that the moon reflects the light of the sun. Many of the constellations were names from Greek mythology.

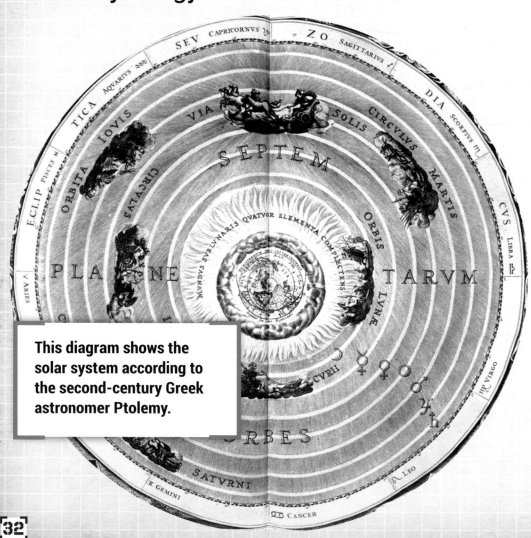

This diagram shows the solar system according to the second-century Greek astronomer Ptolemy.

This medieval illustration shows the goddess of astronomy instructing Ptolemy about the heavens above him.

The ancient Greek scientist and natural philosopher Thales of Miletus (c.624–545 B.C.E.) visited Egypt in 600 B.C.E. He returned with a knowledge of Babylonian astronomy and math. Introducing math to the study of the planets and stars was a breakthrough in astronomy.

HEAVENLY BODIES

The early Greeks had thought that the heavenly bodies were gods who controlled life on Earth. Anaxagoras (c.500–428 B.C.E.) was the first person to suggest that the sun was not actually a god, but was a burning mass of metal. Once the Greeks stopped thinking of heavenly bodies as gods, they started to calculate the movements of the planets and stars. This allowed them to predict the changing seasons, which was of vital help for sailors and farmers.

TECHNICAL SPECS

» The Greeks understood orbits. Each month they saw the moon apparently shrink and then grow, which was unlikely. They reasoned something was passing in front of it.

» Astronomers knew about the planets Mercury, Venus, Mars, Jupiter, and Saturn.

» Aristarchus of Samos (3rd century B.C.E.) suggested that Earth rotates on its axis and the sun is stationary, both of which were proved true centuries later.

» Eratosthenes of Cyrene (3rd century B.C.E.) worked out the circumference of Earth as 29,206 miles (47,000 km). The correct figure is actually 24,902 miles (40,075 km).

TIMING TIME

Ancient civilizations needed to know when the seasons would change so that they knew when to plant and harvest their crops. In the ninth century B.C.E., the poet Hesiod noted that the cry of migrating cranes was a sign that it was time for farmers to plow and sow. Beyond that, each Greek city-state came up with its own annual calendar.

Discovered in an ancient shipwreck, the Antikythera mechanism was made about 100 B.C.E. to calculate the movement of heavenly bodies.

ADVANCED WATER CLOCK

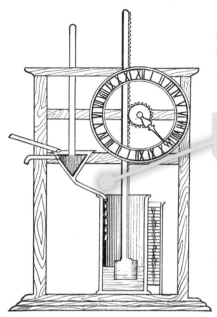

In this water clock, a float rising in the main tank of water raises a toothed rod, which turns a toothed cog to rotate the hand on a clockface, indicating the passage of time.

Water supply drips into tank, raising float

TECHNICAL SPECS

» A Greek day went from sunset to sunset (not midnight to midnight as our day goes).

» Like other ancient cultures, the Greeks had 12 hours of daylight and 12 of night.

» From the 5th to the middle of the 4th century B.C.E. the ancient Greeks divided their year into 12 months with a 13th month added to balance the cycle every eight years.

» Different states started their years at different times. The Athenians kept three calendars. One was for religious festivals. The second was political. The third was astronomical.

» A water clock invented by Ctesibius of Alexandria in 270 B.C.E. used valves to drive ringing bells, moving puppets, and singing birds.

The first water clocks were pottery jars with holes for water to drip through. A large public water clock in Athens, however, had a marker on the outside to show the time. Later clocks were more intricate. Andronichos designed the "tower of the winds" in the first century B.C.E. A complicated water clock gave the time on the sundial on top of the tower, while a rotating disk showed the movements of the stars and the course of the sun through the constellations.

COINS AND COINAGE

The early ancient Greeks exchanged goods and services for other goods they needed. By 600 B.C.E., trade was growing and people began to pay each other with coins. The first coins were lumps of precious metal. Precious metals were common. The silver mine at Laurium made Athens wealthy.

The tunnels in Greek silver mines could be as deep as 330 feet (100 m) and working conditions were extremely harsh. Slaves worked in the mines, using picks and iron hammers to extract the ore.

This silver coin was minted in Athens in the fifth century B.C.E. It features an owl, the symbol of Athena, goddess of wisdom.

EARLY COINAGE

The first coins in Greece were made from electrum, an alloy of gold and silver. From the sixth century B.C.E., the usual metal for coins was pure silver. Each city-state had its own coinage. Athenian silver coins were stamped with an owl. It was the symbol of wisdom and of Athena, the goddess of the city.

MONEY EXCHANGE AND BANKING

As the number of coins in circulation increased, industries developed that were based on money. Money exchange and banking became common professions in the late fifth century B.C.E.

TECHNICAL SPECS

» Coinage was introduced into Greece from Lydia in Asia Minor (modern-day Turkey).

» In ancient Athens, a skilled worker earned one silver drachma per day; one-sixth of a drachma was an obol.

» Pure gold coins were only used after the fourth century B.C.E. Less valuable bronze coins appeared at the end of the fifth century B.C.E.

» Since coinage was a mark of independence, every city had its own mint.

» Greek mines included not just the silver mine at Laurium, but also iron, gold, and copper mines.

A gold coin featuring the head of Alexander the Great, king of the ancient Greek kingdom of Macedon.

MEDICINE

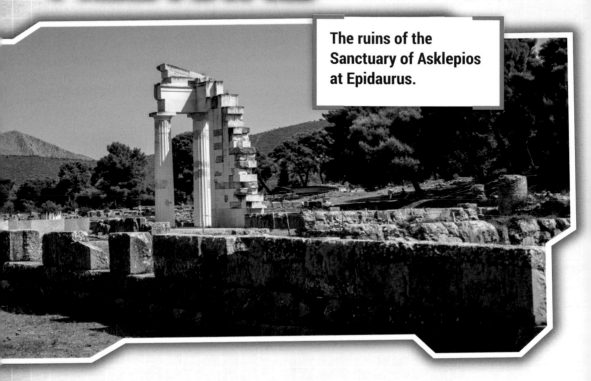

The ruins of the Sanctuary of Asklepios at Epidaurus.

The ancient Greeks believed that sickness could be caused by the gods. However, they also began to realize that good health was also dependent on a person's behavior, environment, and diet. For this reason, Greek medicine combined two types of treatment: one based on magic, and the other on examination and treatment.

The Greek god of medicine and healing was Asklepios, one of the sons of Apollo, the head of the gods. Healing took place in his temples. Greeks went to sleep there when they were sick, or left gifts for the gods.

The Greeks believed Asklepios appeared in a "magical dream," in which he prescribed treatments such as herbal remedies, diets, and exercise. The following day, priests at the temple would administer these cures.

HIPPOCRATES

The cult of Asklepios led to the development of medical treatments for all kinds of diseases. The greatest medical advances came in the Hellenistic period (323–30 B.C.E.), but the most influential doctor was Hippocrates (c.460–c.370 B.C.F.). He was the first to describe the clubbing of fingers (when fingers go purple), which is a sign of lung disease.

TECHNICAL SPECS

» In 400 B.C.E., Hippocrates wrote down rules about how a physician should treat a patient. Physicians still swear the Hippocratic Oath before they can practice medicine.

» Physicians tried to avoid surgery, because they saw that after surgery patients became sick due to shock, loss of blood, or infection.

» The Greeks were the first people to make sure that all their cities had public fountains to supply citizens with clean water for health and sanitation.

» The first medical school opened at Cnidus around 700 B.C.E. There, physicians learned to observe their patients' symptoms.

» Alcmaeon, who wrote the first study of human anatomy between about 500 and 450 B.C.E., worked at the medical school at Cnidus.

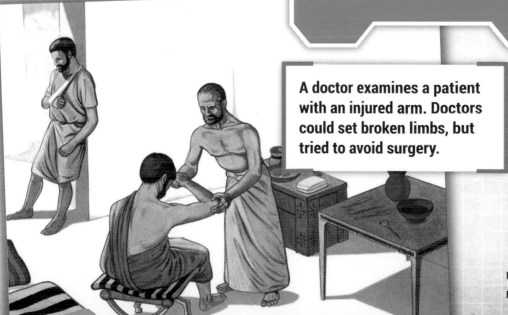

A doctor examines a patient with an injured arm. Doctors could set broken limbs, but tried to avoid surgery.

POTTERY

An Athenian potter shapes a vessel on a wheel. Pottery was normally made and painted by different people.

Pottery is one of the best sources of information about daily life in ancient Greece 2,000 years ago. The Greeks decorated their pottery with all kinds of scenes, and while few paintings and little writing have survived, archaeologists have found many pots and fragments of pottery.

It was easier to show detail in red-figure technique.

The earliest Greek pots were decorated with geometric patterns. In the seventh century B.C.E., potters in Corinth began making pots decorated with black figures.

RED FIGURES

The peak of ancient Greek pottery was the Athenian period from the sixth to fourth centuries B.C.E. In the black-figure technique they painted figures on red clay in special slip (wet clay) that turned black during firing. Around 530 B.C.E., the red-figure technique was introduced. Now it was the pot that turned black and the areas that were unslipped showed through as red figures.

TECHNICAL SPECS

» Larger pots were made in stages using a potter's wheel. The neck and body were thrown separately and joined together. The feet and handles were attached later.

» Ancient Greek pots were fired in three stages. In the first stage, air was let into the kiln. This turned the whole vessel the color of the red clay. Next, green wood was burned to reduce the oxygen supply. The pot turned black in the smoke. In the final stage, air was reintroduced to the kiln; unpainted areas turned back to red, while the painted areas remained black.

» There were specific vessels for carrying food and wine (amphora), drawing water (hydria), and for drinking water and wine (kantharos or kylix).

» The metallic glaze of the black slip was made by using illitic clay, which had low calcium oxide and was collected from local clay beds.

GLASSMAKING

Like the ancient Egyptians and Romans, the ancient Greeks prized glassware. They did not know about glassblowing until late in their history. Instead, the early Greeks produced glassware using clay molds. As glassmakers became more skilled, the vessels became larger and their shapes more complex.

These glass vessels were made near the end of the ancient Greek period, in about the fifth century C.E.

This fourth-century B.C.E. glass vial has two handles so it can be lifted to the mouth for drinking.

The Mesopotamians first made glass around 3500 B.C.E. from a mixture of quartz sand (silica), soda, and lime. Like them, the early Greeks made glassware using the core method. Hot liquid glass was poured over a clay core. When the glass was cool, the core was scraped out.

COLORED GLASS

Later, the Greeks poured viscous glass into molds. To make multicolored glass, threads of glass colored by adding oxides were shaped around the mold. This method was used to make dishes and beads, and for containers such as amphorae. Handles and feet were added later. As well as colored glass, ancient Greeks prized colorless glass. It was difficult to make as it needed to be made of pure silica, which required much higher temperatures to melt it properly. Glass was easier to clean than pottery vessels, and did not taint food as bronze vessels did.

TECHNICAL SPECS

» Glass was almost as precious as gold in ancient Greece.

» There were three terms for glass: "kyanos" referred to dark blue, shiny material, "lithos chyte" meant molten stone, and "hyalos" was everyday glass.

» Glass was present in ancient Mycenae, but no workshops have so far been discovered.

» Historians think there was a substantial glass workshop on the island of Rhodes.

» Glass to be used for mosaics was cast in a flat, open mold and then cut into pieces.

» During the Hellenistic period, thin layers of gold were put between layers of transparent glass. Craftsmen also made cameo, a kind of light-colored glass on a dark glass background.

TIMELINE

B.C.E.

c.1100	The Dark Ages begin in Greece as the Mycenaean civilization declines and the Dorians and Ionians invade.
c.800	The Greeks develop vowels to use with consonants taken from the Phoenician alphabet.
776	The first Olympic Games are held.
c.700	Gold coins are used as money in Lydia in western Anatolia (Turkey).
c.700	Glaucus of Chios is said to learn how to solder iron together.
c.650	The trireme replaces the bireme as the standard Greek warship.
c.600	Thales of Miletus introduces Babylonian math to Greece.
c.600	Sundials are used to measure time.
c.600	Theodorus of Samos is said to invent smelting ores and casting metals.
c.600	Alcmaeon writes the first book on human anatomy.
c.585	Thales of Miletus predicts a solar eclipse.
c.530	Among other discoveries, Pythagoras proposes that musical intervals are based on math, and that sound is a vibration in the air.
c.479	Athens begins a golden age that lasts until 431 B.C.E.
c.450	Anaxagoras of Athens explains eclipses by proposing that the moon reflects sunlight, and has no illumination of its own.
c.440	The lost wax process is used for casting objects in bronze.
c.440	Hippocrates argues that diseases have natural rather than supernatural causes.

c.425	The Thebans are said to use a flamethrower in an attack on Delium.
399	Engineers at Syracuse invent an arrow-firing catapult to defend the city.
387	Plato founds his Academy in Athens.
c.375	Archytas of Tarentum builds the first automaton (robot) and studies mechanics.
c.340	Praxagoras of Crete discovers the difference between veins and arteries.
c.335	Aristotle founds the Lyceum in Athens.
c.330	Aristotle uses the camera obscura to study projection.
327	Alexander the Great of Macedon begins his campaigns of conquest.
c.300	Euclid writes *Elements*, for centuries a standard work on geometry.
c.280	The Pharos of Alexandria is built; it is the world's first lighthouse.
c.270	Ctesibius of Alexandria invents a water clock that uses mechanical gears.
c.245	The library of Alexandria is cataloged for the first time.
c.240	Eratosthenes of Cyrene calculates the diameter of Earth.
c.225	Archimedes invents the Archimedes screw.
c.170	Parchment is invented in Pergamon; it replaces papyrus as writing material.
c.134	Hipparchus measures the year more accurately than anyone before him.

C.E.

45	Sosigenes of Alexandria devises a calendar of 365.25 days, which is adopted by the Roman emperor Julius Caesar (the Julian calendar).
60	Heron of Alexandria builds the first steam engine, and describes many automata.

GLOSSARY

acoustics The science of sound.

acropolis Greek for "high city;" a fortified part of a city on a height. The most famous acropolis was at Athens.

amphora A jar with a long neck and two handles.

city–state A city that governs itself and the surrounding territory.

crop rotation Varying the crops grown in fields to give the soil a chance to recover.

displacement The action by which an object put into water moves away an equal volume of water.

eclipse When one heavenly body passes in front of another.

frieze In architecture, a band of carved decoration, often around the top of a building.

Hellenistic Related to classical Greece.

helmsman The person in charge of steering a ship.

hoplite A Greek foot soldier.

irrigation Artificially watering the land to grow crops.

mosaic Decoration made using small pieces of colored glass or ceramic tile to cover a surface.

orchestra A semicircular space for performances in a Greek theater.

ore Rocks and minerals in which metals naturally occur.

papyrus A type of paper made from the papyrus plant.

phalanx A defensive formation of soldiers with overlapping shields.

philosophy An attempt to understand the world through observation, logical thought, and deduction.

slip A mixture of clay and water used for decorating pots.

staple A food that makes up the major part of a diet.

theorem A mathematical proposal that can be shown to be true.

trireme A warship with three banks of oars.

FURTHER RESOURCES

BOOKS

Bell, Samantha S. *Ancient Greece* (Civilizations of the World). North Star Editions, 2022.

DK. *Eyewitness Ancient Greece* (DK Eyewitness). DK Children, 2023.

Finan, Catherine C. *Ancient Greece* (X-treme Facts: Ancient History). Bearport Pub Co Inc, 2021.

Green, Sara. *Ancient Greece* (Ancient Civilizations). Bellwether Media, 2020.

Levy, Janey. *The Achievements of Ancient Greece* (That's Ancient!). Gareth Stevens Publishing, 2021.

Malam, John. *Ancient Greece Inside Out* (Ancient Worlds Inside Out). Crabtree Publishing, 2017.

WEBSITES

www.ducksters.com/ history/ancient_greece/ science_and_technology. php
Pages on science and technology in ancient Greece, with links to other pages on culture, art, and daily life.

www.primaryresources. co.uk/history/history5b. htm
Primarysources.com page with links to ancient Greek subjects.

greece.mrdonn.org/ philosophy.html
Pages about ancient Greek philosophers and much more from Mr. Donn.

INDEX